CELEBRATING THE FAMILY NAME OF MA

Celebrating the Family Name of Ma

Walter the Educator

Silent King Books
a WhichHead Entertainment Imprint

Copyright © 2024 by Walter the Educator

All rights reserved. No part of this book may be reproduced in any manner whatsoever without written permission except in the case of brief quotations embodied in critical articles and reviews.

First Printing, 2024

Disclaimer

This book is a literary work; the story is not about specific persons, locations, situations, and/or circumstances unless mentioned in a historical context. Any resemblance to real persons, locations, situations, and/or circumstances is coincidental. This book is for entertainment and informational purposes only. The author and publisher offer this information without warranties expressed or implied. No matter the grounds, neither the author nor the publisher will be accountable for any losses, injuries, or other damages caused by the reader's use of this book. The use of this book acknowledges an understanding and acceptance of this disclaimer.

Celebrating the Family Name of Ma is a memory book that belongs to the Celebrating Family Name Book Series by Walter the Educator. Collect them all and more books at WaltertheEducator.com

USE THE EXTRA SPACE TO DOCUMENT YOUR FAMILY MEMORIES THROUGHOUT THE YEARS

MA

Ma, a name of gentle grace,

Rooted deep in time and space.

A lineage vast, both strong and wise,

Its spirit soars, it never dies.

Through valleys lush and rivers wide,

The name Ma flows, a faithful guide.

A whisper soft, a steady tone,

A family's pride, a strength well-known.

In ancient scrolls and village lore,

The Ma name shines forevermore.

A story told through heart and hand,

A legacy rich, a name that stands.

Like bamboo swaying, firm yet kind,

The Ma name carries a steadfast mind.

Through changing winds and shifting tides,

Its honor and truth forever abide.

In fields of art or halls of thought,

The Ma name thrives in all it's sought.

With every step, with every deed,

It plants the roots of future seeds.

The horse that gallops free and strong,

The Ma name rides where dreams belong.

With courage vast and vision clear,

It blazes trails year after year.

From bustling towns to mountain's crest,

The Ma name journeys, seeking the best.

Its legacy built on love and care,

A symbol of hope, beyond compare.

The Ma name bridges earth and sky,

A constant star, it won't deny.

Its melody sweet, its rhythm sure,

A bond unbroken, steadfast, pure.

Through every era, every land,

The Ma name builds with steady hand.

A family strong, a name of pride,

Its strength and spirit never subside.

So here's to Ma, a name renowned,

With roots so deep, with hearts unbound.

A timeless tale of love and light,

Forever shining, day and night.

ABOUT THE CREATOR

Walter the Educator is one of the pseudonyms for Walter Anderson. Formally educated in Chemistry, Business, and Education, he is an educator, an author, a diverse entrepreneur, and he is the son of a disabled war veteran. "Walter the Educator" shares his time between educating and creating. He holds interests and owns several creative projects that entertain, enlighten, enhance, and educate, hoping to inspire and motivate you. Follow, find new works, and stay up to date with Walter the Educator™

at WaltertheEducator.com

www.ingramcontent.com/pod-product-compliance
Lightning Source LLC
LaVergne TN
LVHW012051070526
838201LV00082B/3917